LISTEN TO LITTY . . .

To order additional copies of this book, contact:
Xlibris
1-888-795-4274
www.Xlibris.com
Orders@Xlibris.com

LISTEN TO LITTY...

A BOOK BY LINDA "LITTY" BONANNO
EDITED BY LARONA MCVITIE
PHOTOS BY JONATHAN ORTIZ
GRAPHIC DESIGN BY NEIL SEEJOOR

It's never too early to learn about healthy living...

Stay pretty and let Litty plant the seed of prevention with easy tips as you grow into a beautiful "inside out" young lady!

LISTEN TO LITTY...
A BOOK BY LINDA BONANNO

Dedicated to Sienna Hope...may you dance into a bright future!

#mymusic

#myhealth

#myfitness

#mynutrition

#myfashion

#mydance

#myenvironment

#myspirituality

#mycommunity

#myprofession

#mybeauty

M
Y
H
E
A
L
T
H

LITTY says...

- **Litty's Motto:** PREVENTION STARTS WITH YOU, GO AHEAD AND MAKE A MOVE!

- **Litty's To Do List:** ASK MOMMY AND DADDY ABOUT YOUR FAMILY HEALTH HISTORY AND FIND OUT MORE ABOUT YOUR BODY AND HOW TO PROTECT YOURSELF!

- **Listen to Litty Boys and Girls:** KNOWLEDGE IS POWER AND **HEALTH IS WEALTH!**

HELP LITTY PREVENT BREAST CANCER!!

MY ENVIRONMENT

LITTY says...

- **Litty's Motto:** A SAFE ENVIRONMENT HELPS PREVENT MANY ILLNESSES!

- **Litty's To Do List: AVOID ALL THESE BAD GUYS:** TOXIC CHEMICALS FOUND IN SOME PLASTIC AND STYROFOAM, SOME CLEANING SUPPLIES, SOME BEAUTY CARE AND FRAGRANCES, CERTAIN FOODS (PESTICIDES & GMOs) AND RADIATION FROM LAPTOPS AND PHONES.

- **Listen to Litty Boys and Girls:** YOUR BODY AND YOUR SKIN ABSORBS EVERYTHING. **CAREFULLY READ ALL PRODUCT LABELS.**

M
Y

N
U
T
R
I
T
I
O
N

LITTY says...

- **Litty's Motto:** YOU ARE WHAT YOU EAT!

- **Litty's To Do List:** CHOOSING A HEALTHY DIET LOW IN FAT AND SUGAR, HIGH IN VEGETABLES AND FIBER CAN GREATLY HELP REDUCE MANY DISEASES.

- **Listen to Litty Boys and Girls:** CLEAN FOODS HAVE FRESH INGREDIENTS; READ YOUR LABELS CAREFULLY AND **ALWAYS PICK ORGANIC AND UNPROCESSED FOODS.**

M
Y

F
I
T
N
E
S
S

LITTY says…

- **Litty's Motto:** EAT-ACTION-SLEEP-REPEAT!!

- **Litty's To Do List:** EAT CLEAN, STAY ACTIVE, KEEP YOUR BODY HYRDRATED BY DRINKING LOTS OF WATER AND GETTING LOTS OF REST. THESE ARE THE BEST WAYS TO REMAIN HEALTHY.

- **Listen to Litty Boys and Girls:** RID YOUR BODY OF TOXINS BY EXERCISING… **1,2,3…GET MOVING REGULARLY!**

M Y   S P I R I T U A L I T Y

LITTY says...

- **Litty's Motto:** IT'S TIME TO BEAUTIFY YOUR SOUL, MAKE THAT YOUR LIFETIME GOAL!

- **Litty's To Do List:** BE SPIRITUAL AND CONNECT WITH YOURSELF AND THE UNIVERSE SO YOU CAN IMPROVE YOUR HEALTH BY LOWERING YOUR STRESS AND BRINGING HOPE AND HAPPINESS TO YOUR LIFE.

- **Listen to Litty Boys and Girls:** SPREAD LOVE, ACCEPTANCE, COMPASSION AND REMEMBER TO **ALWAYS BE GRUDGE FREE!**

M Y   P R O F E S S I O N

LITTY says...

- **Litty's <u>Motto</u>:** A PERSON WITH PURPOSE IS A HEALTHY PERSON!

- **Litty's <u>To Do List</u>:** BECOME A YOUNG ENTREPRENEUR BY GETTING OUT OF YOUR COMFORT ZONE, BY BEING HONEST AND RELIABLE, SELF MOTIVATING, HARD WORKING AND ALWAYS EAGER TO LEARN.

- **<u>Listen to Litty Boys and Girls</u>:** ALWAYS SOLVE PROBLEMS WITH COMMUNICATION AND KNOW THAT **TIME IS YOUR BIGGEST ASSET!**

**M
Y

M
U
S
I
C**

LITTY says...

- **Litty's <u>Motto:</u>** LET MUSIC BE YOUR MEDICINE!

- **Litty's <u>To Do List:</u>** USE THE HEALING POWER OF MUSIC TO REMAIN RELAXED, ENTERTAINED, STRESS–FREE AND KEEP YOUR IMMUNE SYSTEM WORKING AND HEALTHY ALL AROUND.

- **<u>Listen to Litty Boys and Girls:</u>** MAKE MUSIC YOUR BEST FRIEND AND **LET YOUR FAVORITE MELODY BRING OUT THE BEST IN YOU!**

M Y D A N C E

LITTY says...

- **<u>Litty's Motto:</u>** EXPRESS YOURSELF THROUGH DANCE AND FIND PEACE!

- **<u>Litty's To Do List:</u>** LET DANCE IMPROVE YOUR MUSCLES, BONES, BREATHING, CIRCULATION AND MOOD WHILE BUILDING CONFIDENCE, DISCIPLINE, BODY AWARENESS AND CREATIVITY.

- **<u>Listen to Litty Boys and Girls:</u>** DANCE AWAY WITH PASSION AND **KEEP A HEALTHY CONNECTION BETWEEN YOUR BODY, MIND AND SOUL WITH THE POWER OF DANCE!**

M
Y

B
E
A
U
T
Y

LITTY says...

- **Litty's <u>Motto:</u>** BEAUTY IS TAKING CARE OF YOURSELF IN EVERY WAY!

- **Litty's <u>To Do List:</u>** SHOWER REGULARLY, WEAR CLEAN CLOTHING, WASH YOUR FACE AND BRUSH YOUR TEETH TWICE DAILY. HYGIENE IS IMPORTANT IN KEEPING A GOOD APPEARANCE.

- <u>**Listen to Litty Boys and Girls:**</u> SMILE OFTEN! DON'T HIDE BEHIND A MASK. **BE YOURSELF TO BE BEAUTIFUL AND HEALTHY INSIDE AND OUT.**

M Y

F A S H I O N

LITTY says...

- <u>Litty's **Motto:**</u> WHEN YOU LOOK GOOD YOU FEEL GOOD!

- <u>Litty's **To Do List:**</u> **LITTY'S SECRET RECIPE:** TWO CUPS OF SELF CONFIDENCE, A SPRINKLE OF LAUGHTER, TOP IT ALL OFF WITH YOUR PERSONAL FASHIONISTA INGREDIENTS, THE ACCESSORIES YOU LOVE AND THERE YOU HAVE IT, YOU GOT STYLE!

- <u>Listen to Litty **Boys and Girls:**</u> EXPRESS YOURSELF WITH FASHION AND **LET YOUR UNIQUE STYLE MAKE YOU A STAR!**

M Y

C O M M U N I T Y

LITTY says...

- **Litty's Motto**: UNITED WE STAND! EVERYONE DESERVES A CHANCE!

- **Litty's To Do List**: BE A LEADER AND BE A PART OF PROGRESS BY HELPING MAKE CHANGES IN YOUR COMMUNITY.

- **Listen to Litty Boys and Girls:** LET YOUR PURPOSE SERVICE OTHERS AND MAKE THE WORLD AROUND YOU A BETTER PLACE. **YOU ARE THE FUTURE!**

27

Draw with Litty...

Draw with Litty...

Printed in the United States
By Bookmasters